A

THE
DATING
PROJECT

JASON & CRYSTALINA **EVERT**

ASCENSION

West Chester, Pennsylvania

Copyright © 2018 Ascension Publishing, LLC.
All rights reserved.

With the exception of short excerpts used in articles and critical reviews, no part of this work may be reproduced, transmitted, or stored in any form whatsoever, printed or electronic, without the prior written permission of the publisher.

Ascension Press
Post Office Box 1990
West Chester, PA 19380
1-800-376-0520
ascensionpress.com

Cover design by Joseph Montfort
Printed in the United States of America
ISBN 978-1-945179-52-5

CONTENTS

How to Use This Guide iv

Introduction 1

Discussion Questions 8

Top Ten Dating Tips 20

What Are Your Intentions? 32

Look at Me, Notice Me 37

Guys, Here's How to Ask a Girl on a Date 41

Dating with Detachment 46

Going from "Friends" to "More Than Friends" 53

The Worst Thing She Could Say Is No 59

Dealing with Rejection 66

Why I Don't Date Men Who Are "Willing" to Save Sex 69

Four Helpful Rules for Discernment 75

The Dating Assignment 80

Dating Journal 82

Dating Resources from the Authors 90

Acknowledgements 92

HOW TO USE THIS GUIDE

This Guide has been designed as the perfect companion to the award-winning *Dating Project* film from Pure Flix. It includes thought-provoking, conversation-starting discussion questions and related articles, as well as Boston College professor Kerry Cronin's very popular "dating assignment."

The discussion questions are broken out by category with plenty of space for journaling and note-taking. This makes for easy group study or personal reflection at home, on campus, or in the classroom. The "dating assignment" also includes space to write out action plans and to record the results.

Since the film is only an hour in length, we recommend watching it in one sitting. The questions, however, are substantial enough to allow for multiple sessions, depending on the needs of a particular individual or group. So, if you prefer more than one session, simply watch the film in one session, then tackle a couple of the question categories at each subsequent gathering.

If you are studying the film in a group setting, be sure each participant has his or her own Guide to make the most of the experience.

INTRODUCTION

We live in a culture where single people act like they're dating, dating couples behave like they're married, and married people live like they're single . . . and we somehow do all of this without asking anyone out on a date!

It's time to get things back in order.

For the first time in history, the majority of Americans are unmarried. Among all these singles, it would seem that a third of them are in a relationship, a third are not, and the other third do not even know if they are dating or not dating.

Have relationships always been so confusing? The answer is no. For proof, we offer for your consideration a letter we received from an elderly woman describing what dating was like in the 1940s (handwritten on her powdery blue stationery with clouds and a rainbow). She described herself as a "lively nursing student" in San Diego in the 1940s. She recalled her college life:

All of us were constantly and happily "dating" young navy and marine men. In those days, chastity was a given. Most of us received many more than one or two marriage proposals. Going back to when I first started dating in 1940, by 1945 my own count was a ten. All during 1946, the days past graduation were followed by marriages for almost all of us in our fifteen-person class. These were marriages that lasted through our lifetimes.

Not long after her 50th wedding anniversary, her husband became ill. After years of caring for him with the tenderness of a bride, she held him as he "passed peacefully away in my arms" on February 13th.

A date every weekend to go dancing with men in uniform? Ten wedding proposals in five years, a fifty-five-year marriage, and holding her lover as he passed into eternal life . . . on the eve of Valentine's Day?

Not bad. In fact, it sounds even better than swiping across a dating app.

It's hard to believe that less than a century ago, men considered chastity to be "a given" and leapt at the chance to offer women their hand in marriage. Nowadays some people are frustrated if the other expects so much as a text message after a hookup.

This woman's experience was not the exception. It was the norm. We met another grandmother who said that her mom advised her never to go on a date with the same man two weekends in a row but to let other guys take her out. Otherwise, she said, "if you let the same man take you out on consecutive dates, it might make him think you're interested. Don't do that. Let them wonder."

What planet did these women live on? Nowadays, many women would be satisfied if two men asked them out in one year. Something has shifted, and people are becoming increasingly unsettled about it. In a recent *Vanity Fair* article titled "Tinder and the Dawn of the Dating Apocalypse," the author interviewed a number of women regarding their assessment of the modern dating scene. Here's what they felt:

"It's rare for a woman of our generation to meet a man who treats her like a priority instead of an option." – Erika

"There is no dating. There's no relationships. They're rare. You can have a fling that could last like seven, eight months and you could never actually call someone your 'boyfriend.' [Hooking up] is a lot easier. No one gets hurt—well, not on the surface. . . . It's a contest to see who cares less, and guys win a lot at caring less. But if you say any of this out loud, it's like you're weak, you're not independent, you somehow missed the whole memo about third-wave feminism." – Amanda

But it's not only the women who are dissatisfied with the status of modern relationships. The American Psychological Association published a nationwide study entitled "Sexual Hookup Culture: A Review." In it, they not only mentioned that college students overestimate the sexual activity of their peers, they also noted that those who were hooking up were not very satisfied with the outcome. Only 5% of students reported feeling proud during a hookup, and only 2% felt desirable or wanted after a hookup. Although 63% of college-aged men said they would prefer a traditional romantic relationship to a hookup, they hook up twice as frequently as they go on first dates. In fact, more than 90% of "friends with benefits" relationships never evolve into committed relationships.

Donna Freitas remarked, "Students, in theory, will acknowledge that a hookup can be good. But I think they also experience the hookup as something they need to prove, that they can be sexually intimate with someone and then walk away not caring about that person or what they did. It's a very callous attitude toward sexual experiences. But it seems like many students go into the hookup aware of this social contract, but then come out of it unable to uphold it and realizing that they do have feelings about what happened. They end up feeling ashamed that they can't be callous."

In healthy dating relationships, the heart does not need to be divorced from the body. And this is only one difference between hooking up and chaste dating. Consider the twenty differences listed on the next page.

If a hookup fails to satisfy, why do so many settle for it? It's fair to say that just wanting to reach a destination does not mean a person knows how to navigate there. Many people want love, but they don't know how to get there.

What is needed is a dating revolution with a clear map for how to pursue authentic love. As idyllic as our grandmothers' experiences might seem, though, the goal of modern men and women should not be to roll back history. We need to move forward but in a way that gleans from previous generations the principles that allowed dating experiences to be purposeful and successful.

HOOKUP	CHASTE DATING
No emotional attachment	Open to attachment
Always short term	Possibility of forever
Rushed	No rush
Lustful	Loving
Purely physical (pleasure is the desire)	Deeper than physical (you are the desire)
Hidden from the family	Open to family guidance
No commitment	Committed
Potential for physical harm	Safe
Usually done under the influence	Sober and clean
Standards must be lowered	No moral compromise required
Other is seen as someone to be used	Other is seen as someone to be loved
Clouds one's judgment of the other	Opens one's eyes to the other
Regret	Hope
Emotionally damaging	Emotionally fulfilling
Driven by impatience and selfishness	Initiated by hope and self-giving
Relationship undefined	Relationship defined
No respect	Respect
Requires one only to submit to passion	Requires effort and a sincere pursuit
Dignity diminished	Dignity intact
Requires consent (sometimes)	Requires courage (always)

In *The Dating Project*, Professor Cronin
offers a simple set of rules:
(For the full dating assignment, see page 80.)

THE RULES:

1. Ask someone out *in person* who is a legitimate romantic interest.
2. Keep the date simple: 60-90 minutes.
3. The date cannot involve drugs or alcohol.
4. Don't express physical intimacy beyond a simple hug.
5. You ask, you pay.
6. Think of 3-4 questions before the date.

What's great about her approach is its simplicity. The challenge is doing it. Therefore, we've assembled a team of authors to create this study guide to help you implement these rules in a way that can hopefully lead you to a lifetime of love.

DISCUSSION QUESTIONS

DATING IS...

1. What do you think about "The Rules" Professor Cronin offers?

2. Which of the rules do you feel is the most difficult?

3. Complete this sentence: Dating today is...

4. One man in the film noted that when you take a woman on a date, you should take her *out*, instead of inviting her to come over and watch Netflix. What do you think is the importance of taking people "out" rather than taking them "in"?

5. The film noted that many young people don't know how to date because they don't know how to ask the other person out. What are some specific ways you could ask someone out? What are ways that you would like to be asked out?

6. Many people are not sure what to talk about on a date. What are things that you think are good to discuss on a first date?

7. List five great first date ideas.

8. Shanzi noted, "I feel like everyone secretly wants to date, but no one is willing to say it." Why do you think no one is willing to admit this?

9. Cecilia mentioned that a man once said to her, "We're dating, but we're not dating dating." What would you do if you found yourself in a quasi-relationship with someone who didn't feel like defining your status?

HOOKUP CULTURE

1. Professor Cronin remarked that hooking up has become more casual than a cup of coffee, and Shanzi added that asking someone on a date is a much bigger deal than hooking up. Describe why you think this has happened.

2. In what ways do you think the fear of commitment and the fear of rejection have fueled the hookup culture?

3. Professor Cronin noted the ambiguity of the term "hookup." What do you think would happen in culture if such vague words did not exist and people could only describe their actions with specific words?

4. One young man in the video noted that asking someone out on a date "already trumps any feeling you could have hooking up." Why do you think he felt that way?

5. Cecilia stated that any sign of physical affection felt weird after not experiencing it for so long. For many people involved in the hookup culture, do you think the root cause has more to do with loneliness or lust?

6. If people experienced more healthy affection, human interaction, and intimacy, what do you think would happen to the rates of hooking up? Would there be less of a "feast" if there wasn't so much of a "famine"?

7. One of Professor Cronin's rules for a Level 1 date is sobriety. If society recognizes the danger of drinking and driving, why do you think so few recognize the danger of drinking and dating?

8. Although Shanzi admitted she succumbed to hookup culture, she realized, "I can change right now." What specific things can a person do in order to start over, regardless of the past?

9. Professor Cronin taught her students that the hookup culture is alluring because everyone is looking for self-worth, and it is difficult to hold on to self-worth because it gets worn down by the world. What can a person do in order to build up self-worth without devaluing oneself in the process?

ARE YOU READY TO DATE?

1. Chris felt that the dating pool is a "competitive market . . . it's sales." But he added, "I haven't stocked what I'm selling." If you were to take an inventory of your personal life, what items do you feel you need to begin stocking? In other words, are there areas of your life that you know you need to change in order to prepare for your vocation?

2. Many people fear commitment. Chris noted, "The impulse is a lack of freedom . . . I lose something in a commitment. The fear of that is then I have to start getting my stuff together." Describe some of the reasons why people today are afraid to give of themselves.

3. Later in the film, Chris admitted, "When I started this [film], I thought of commitment . . . it scared me, and I felt that it was limited. Commitment limits me in a sense, but it makes me go deep. And that actually makes me feel stronger and feel more authentic." In what ways does a person find himself or herself through a gift of self?

4. Chris lost his father at the age of nine, and he said that he probably would be married with children by now if he had a dad. He said, "I wish I had a mentor. I wish someone would show me the way." When a person is raised without a good example of marriage, how can he or she fill this void in a healthy way?

5. The movie concludes by challenging viewers, "So go on a date, and date differently." But how do you know when you're ready to date? Should this decision involve your friends and family?

PURSUING LOVE

1. Many of the women in *The Dating Project* lamented that men simply do not ask anyone out any more. Reflecting on movies where men pursued women, Shanzi said, "I think it's so cute when guys are pursuing a girl, because guys just went for girls they liked. And it was great, and you felt special. I just want to feel special. I want a guy to pursue me." Why do you think men have stopped asking women out?

2. Rasheeda remarked, "If a man wants you, he is going to pursue you." Part of pursuing a woman is facing the fear of rejection. Do you think it's important for a man to learn how to face these fears in person instead of connecting to women through apps?

3. When it comes to pursuing love, it seems as if a woman is not supposed to be aggressive or passive or passive-aggressive. So, what do you think women can do in order to be actively receptive to finding love? Do you think most women want to be free to ask a guy out? Or, do you feel most would prefer that the man take the initiative?

4. In the film, Lori Gottleib points out that we are intentional about getting a job, but we lack that intentionality in finding a spouse. What can men and women do in the modern culture to be intentional about finding a spouse?

5. In her discussion with Shanzi, Professor Cronin said that when you spend time "crushing" on someone for a while instead of getting to know the person, you end up building up a false idea of who he or she might be. How can men and women exercise better custody of their hearts and imaginations in the early phases of a relationship?

6. Chris shared how he felt loneliness when the phone died, and this emptiness made him realize that he wanted true friendship and connection. In what ways does the superficial connectedness of social media create isolation?

7. When Chris asked his mother, "Do you think it's mostly luck?", she answered, "No I think you have to pray to God and then go by his guidance." Do you pray to God to follow his guidance in your dating relationships, or do you tend to trust your own efforts more than his will? What does it specifically look like to trust him?

WAITING FOR MARRIAGE

1. Rasheeda remarked that people nowadays seem to think that it's unrealistic and old-fashioned to reserve sexual intimacy for marriage. What are some of the benefits that come with self-restraint?

2. In Chris's words, "To be in a dating relationship and not have sex is very difficult. I guess my prayer would be ... that I can be enough of a man to experience that. Because otherwise I'm just a boy." In what ways does self-mastery prepare a man for the demands of love and fidelity in marriage?

3. When Cecilia asked her friends if they would mind if their boyfriends look at porn, one of them replied by comparing cooking shows to porn. What do you think about this analogy? Should fidelity apply only to a person's body, or should it include their imagination and heart as well?

4. Chris said, "I regret being an idiot and being a coward and not being true to myself . . . it's taken a while to grow up . . . If I am looking at the menu all the time, how can I be in a relationship. And I'm realizing, well, that's always going to be there. There's always going to be lust. I got to start managing these thoughts." With all the temptations available, how can a person begin to manage his or her thoughts of lust?

5. Chris's mother noted how many people wonder, "How will I know whether I like her or not unless I sleep with her?" She declared, "That's not what makes a marriage, and that's not what keeps it going. It's the fact that you're willing to sacrifice for that other person." How does premarital sex compromise a person's capacity to sacrifice?

6. When Rasheeda told a man that she has chosen to save sex for marriage, he challenged her on her values, leaving her feeling disappointed in the character of modern men. She explained that when circumstances are bad, she trusts in God and holds on to his promises. What are practical ways you can do this when you feel discouraged?

WHEN IT'S NOT MEANT TO BE

1. Chris said that he sometimes focused on a woman's imperfections and wondered if he was really just "looking for the exit door." He asked, "Why am I so afraid of it?" What do you think was at the root of his fears?

2. In Rasheeda's discussion with her friend, her friend points out two main fears about online dating (disappointment and rejection). In her words, "If you feel like you have to make something work, then it's not for you . . . If you have to chase him, let him go!" What do you think keeps people from letting go when they know they're settling in a relationship?

3. One of the reasons given in the film for why people shield themselves from relationships is because they are afraid of being hurt (or being hurt again). How can a person learn to trust again after having been wounded in past relationships?

4. Chris points out serious questions that one should answer before dating someone, such as what the other thinks about sex, babies, adoption, money, friendship, and religion. He adds, "For me to walk into a relationship and be physical and not know these things is really stupid and selfish." If you find the answers to these serious questions and the other person's values do not align with yours, what should you do?

5. Cecilia had been single for more than five years when her aunt told her, "You're single because you want to be single." As difficult as this may have been to hear, it was true. If Cecilia had lowered her standards enough, she could have had companionship at any moment. But she did not want to settle for false companionship. She was actively waiting for the right person. When tempted to settle for less, what can you do to renew your resolution to hope in real love?

TOP TEN DATING TIPS
BY JASON AND CRYSTALINA EVERT

1. LIVE THE SEASON OF SINGLENESS TO THE FULL

For many singles, the season of life prior to marriage often feels like the forty years Moses spent wandering in the wilderness. The aloneness, combined with uncertainty about the future and regret about the past, often makes this a difficult time to endure. But it does not need to be so difficult. What do you do in the meantime?

Quit living in the future and the past. You only have today.

Make a plan to limit the time you spend on social media. The endless streams of flawless filtered photos make everyone's life seem perfect except for your own. Social media also creates a false sense of connectedness. You might have 10,000 followers, and yet none of them know what kind of day you're having. *The New York Times* noted, "We think constant connection will make us feel less lonely. The opposite is true.

If we are unable to be alone, we are far more likely to be lonely."[1]

Don't obsess about finding the perfect person. Become the person your future spouse deserves and let God take care of the rest.

During this time, develop friendships with potential future mates instead of rushing into romance. By doing this, you can find answers to serious questions, such as...

- How does this person treat people he/she is not attracted to?
- What do his/her exes think about him/her?
- Do I admire this person, or is it merely physical?
- What kind of people does he/she choose as friends?
- Does he/she share my morality or just "respect" it?
- Does he/she make me a better person?

If you build a solid foundation of friendship while living a life of purpose and direction, you are giving your future relationship the best chance to thrive before it even begins.

---

[1] Sherry Turkle, "The Flight From Conversation," *The New York Times*, April 21, 2012.

2. UNDERSTAND THE PURPOSE OF DATING

The main reason why dating has become so confusing is that society has forgotten the point of it. Plain and simple: The purpose of dating is to find a spouse. It is an act of marital discernment, not a passing remedy for loneliness.

Why has the connection between dating and marriage been blurred? One reason is that more singles than ever were raised in divorced households. As a result, an increasing number of people no longer aspire to marriage. A second reason is that expressions of intimacy that had been once reserved for marriage are often exchanged before two people are even dating. As a result, men in particular have become less motivated to enter marriage. They can often get its privileges without needing to accept any of its demands.

If dating is to again become what it should be, two things need to happen. First, singles must have the courage to hope that their parents' broken relationships need not determine the future of their own relationships. Second, the total gift of one's body should be given alongside the total gift of the person in marriage. We are not meant to be given away in pieces. For more on this, see dating tip number nine, below.

Dating is like a highway that only has two exits: breakup or marriage. Therefore, there's no reason to enter a relationship unless you can see yourself possibly marrying him or her.

3. FACE YOUR FEARS

Before entering a relationship, it is essential that men and women face their fears. That means facing the fear of commitment as well as the fear of rejection. Men, in particular, fear initiating a relationship because of the possibility of rejection. They fear committing to a person because someone better might come along. And they fear giving of themselves because they assume they will lose themselves in the process. This fear springs from a bogus idea of freedom that enslaves a man. G.K. Chesterton noted, "Most modern freedom is at root fear. It is not so much that we are too bold to endure rules; it is rather that we are too timid to endure responsibilities."[2]

Meanwhile, many women are afraid that they are simply not worth pursuing. They're either "too much" or they're "not enough." In an effort to avoid being alone, they may lower their standards, justify their decisions, despair that love exists, and settle for being someone's friend with benefits. As they lower the boundaries around their bodies, they build a fortress around their hearts. But if you have to lower your morals in order to find love, then it is not love that you are finding.

Rather than running from commitment or rushing into a hookup, men and women must hold their ground and face their fears.

---

[2] G.K. Chesterton, "Authority the Unavoidable," in *G.K. Chesterton: Collected Works, Volume IV* (Ignatius Press, San Francisco, 1987), 166-167.

4. KNOW WHAT YOU WANT

There is plenty of confusion when it comes to hooking up and modern dating, but there is one thing we don't need to be confused about, and that is our deepest desires. Sometimes singles become so focused on getting into a relationship that they don't ponder what qualities they want in that other person. So, go ahead and make a list! Some items can be fun and negotiable. Others are not debatable. Don't just consider which physical features or personality traits would attract you in a date. Think about the core values and virtues you want a future spouse to possess. Regardless of how attractive another person might be, if that person does not have the most essential qualities you want, then you have no business dating him or her.

Don't be afraid to have standards and non-negotiable boundaries when it comes to dating. Once you have your list, take it seriously. Having this clear set of hopes will provide perspective when you are tempted to lower the bar. This can prevent you from dating the wrong person . . . thus leaving open the door for the right one to walk in!

And, in the meantime, make sure you live up to your own list.

5. DISCERN YOUR DATES

Imagine how many heartbreaks could have been prevented if people took the time to discern their relationships and realize one fact: Just because you experience a mutual attraction with someone, this does not mean that you should date him or her.

Use the chart below to help decide who and when you should be dating.

Right Person Right Time	Right Time Wrong Person
Right Person Wrong Time	Wrong Person Wrong Time

Often, people will choose to date based upon whether they think the other person is right for them. But, they often don't consider if it is the right time to date. Before committing to anyone, you ought to take a sober assessment of your life: "Am I even ready to date? Are there things in my life that I need to root out before I can be a good spouse to someone? Do I need serious healing from vices or wounds that are holding me back?" Facing these questions is real marriage preparation.

In the above chart, you only want to move forward in commitment if it is the right person at the right time. If you find yourself in any of the other three boxes, focus on the friendship.

When you make decisions about relationships, don't discern alone. Make sure you are connected to family and good friends, who can often see things that you cannot. Having the humility to listen to their input will only help you make smarter relationship decisions.

6. LOOK FOR LOVE IN THE RIGHT PLACES

Because it has become so difficult for singles to find one another, technology has stepped in with dating apps and websites to connect potential couples. While many good relationships have bloomed from this, there have also been plenty of disappointed users. So, here are a few principles to keep in mind:

- Be careful to avoid a consumer attitude when you approach online dating. If you feel you are beginning to look at so many profiles that it feels like a human menu, perhaps it's time to take a break and try your luck meeting more people in person.
- While there is such a thing as online meeting, there is no such thing as online dating. That needs to happen in person. If you're looking for a relationship that begins online, try to pursue realistic prospects who don't live on the other side of the galaxy.
- Don't hide your values or pretend to be someone you think the other person wants you to be. What if being fake actually works? At what point does it end?

7. NO MISSIONARY DATING

Have you ever seen one of those home makeover shows where a person falls in love with a run-down property because of all the potential in it? Some people, usually women, are particularly prone to this with dating. They commit to a man who (if he were a house) would be a dilapidated, haunted house, and they think, "Ooh, but I could put new curtains in it and build a swimming pool out back!" Don't do this. Don't date your imagination. You are supposed to date a person, not a project.

Never commit to a person hoping he or she will change. Rather, you want to commit to a person hoping he or she will stay the way they are. Sure, we all have imperfections, but be realistic with yourself about how much you expect the other to change. One good way to decide is to ask yourself: If this person's habit never changes, would I be content to be married for the rest of my life to him/her? If not, then don't do missionary dating.

If you go on a date with someone and you know that he or she is not the right one, don't drag things on because you don't want to hurt them or because you want to change them. Never forget that sometimes a successful date is one where you discover the person is not for you.

8. MAKE COMMITMENT CLEAR

One thing that makes modern dating more confusing than ever is couples' inability to define their relationship status. So, instead of being flirty and hoping for the best, try this:
1. Discern if you should enter a relationship with someone.
2. Pursue them with sincerity.
3. Commit to them with clarity.

Some people never move forward in a relationship because they want absolute certainty that the relationship will work. Don't fall into paralysis by analysis. Discern sufficiently and then move. Relax, it's not a proposal. In the meantime, don't behave like you are dating when you are not.

9. KEEP IT PURE

Just as singles should not behave like they are dating, dating couples should not act like spouses. Not long ago, I saw a meme online that was worth sharing on our social media accounts. Within hours, it had been viewed more than three million times. What was the revolutionary statement it made? Overlaid on a simple photo of a bride and groom, one sentence was written in bold text: "Boyfriends don't get husband privileges, period."

If you recall, in the letter written by the grandmother above, she noted that "chastity was a given." It was taken for granted.

Nowadays, what's taken for granted is the notion that there is only one prerequisite for sexual intimacy: mutual consent. As long as no one is being coerced, what could be wrong?

What's wrong is that during sexual intimacy, the bodies speak a language that says, "I give myself totally to you. I am all yours." But unless the couple is married, then a lie is being spoken through their bodies, even if the couple had no such intention to be dishonest. The total gift of the body (sex) should correspond with the total gift of the person (marriage). Therefore, the topic of sexual purity is really about sexual honesty. We're called to speak the truth not only with our words, but in and through our bodies.

One of the benefits of purity is that it brings the other's intentions to the surface. If he or she is unwilling to wait for you, is it really you that the other is pursuing? As one person said, "Just because a person desires you, does not mean they value you."

Furthermore, giving yourself to the other sexually is no guarantee that the person will be more likely to stay with you. In fact, one man argued for the opposite, saying, "The girls who sleep with me right away and expect me to wife them up always end up disappointed because I simply can't bring myself to respect them enough."

Sometimes couples will look at such a callous attitude and think, "We're different. It's not like this is a meaningless hookup. We're committed, and we've never felt this way about someone else before." But the destiny of one's relationship is not determined by the intensity of one's attractions. It is the willingness to sacrifice that makes love last. In fact, The Economist published the results of a survey of more than 2000 couples and found that those couples who waited the longest to begin having sex—in particular those who waited until marriage—had better communication, were more satisfied in their relationship, felt their relationship was more stable, and reported a higher level of sexual satisfaction within marriage.[3]

10. DON'T STOP DATING WHEN YOU'RE MARRIED

Do you know the real reason why there is a dating crisis among singles? It's because married people forgot how to date. At some point, they stopped chasing each other and began existing together. This is not what marriage is supposed to look like.

A friend of mine has been married for more than fifteen years and has never missed his weekly date night with his wife. That is a man whose children will know how to date. Therefore, when you enter into marriage, don't end your pursuit of one another. It's just the beginning.

---

[3] "Premarital Sex: The Waiting Game," *The Economist*, January 20, 2011.

Jason and Crystalina Evert married in 2003 and have spoken about dating, relationships, and sexuality on six continents to more than one million teens and young adults. They are the authors or co-authors of more than fifteen books, including *How to Find Your Soulmate Without Losing Your Soul*, *If You Really Loved Me*, and *Pure Womanhood*. Jason earned a master's degree in theology and undergraduate degrees in counseling and theology with a minor in philosophy at Franciscan University of Steubenville. He and Crystalina are frequent guests on radio programs throughout the country, and they have appeared on Fox News, MSNBC, the BBC, and EWTN. Crystalina runs the website Women Made New, and together Jason and Crystalina are the co-founders of Chastity Project.

WHAT ARE YOUR INTENTIONS?
BY BOBBY ANGEL

I work at an all-boys' high school, so it's easy to play Socrates and annoy my students with questions. "You believe that you'll never regret that haircut?" "You really think this fidget spinner will stand the test of time, huh?" It's especially easy to provoke them with questions pertaining to romance and dating.

"*Why* exactly are you booking that hotel room after your prom?" "*Why* exactly did you stay up talking with that girl until 4 AM?" "*Why* are you buying that extra-large bouquet of roses and making a mixtape for a girl whose last name you don't know?"

We all have a desire for intimacy, to see another and be seen by them, to know another and be known by them. It is arguably the deepest ache of the human heart, that yearning for communion. But the desire for union can run amok if we're not careful. It takes great practice in self-mastery to learn how to rein in our passions and consistently ask the hard question: *What's going on in my heart?* Recognizing the signs we are sending and being honest in shining a light at our true intentions are great steps in both self-knowledge and learning how to love authentically.

KNOW THYSELF

We can lead people on if we are not careful. Perhaps you have experienced this, either on the giving or receiving end. Maybe you felt really "into" the other person, only to find out that he or she was never totally invested. Maybe you were the one who sent signs and offered some romantic gestures but soon realized that you wanted out, and the other person was crushed.

No one has done this "dating thing" perfectly. I have certainly made my share of mistakes and have led girls on when I was not in a place to give of myself fully. We can all be self-centered and try to fill our interior loneliness or even our lust with another person. Few people do this maliciously, but it doesn't make it right. No one wants to be led on, and we rightly feel horrible when we lead people on. So how do we get out of this loop?

To start, ask the hard questions: *What are my deeper intentions for this person? What do I intend to get out of this date? What are the signs that I have given so far? Have I indicated that I am more invested in this relationship than I really am? Am I even in a place to commit to another person?*

Being honest with yourself is difficult, but it is the necessary starting point in eliminating needless drama or heartache from your relationships. It is also an essential part of growing up.

READ THE SIGNS

Part of the brilliance of *The Dating Project* is its challenge to reclaim a detached form of dating. This dating is a true "getting to know" the other person without the pressure of assuming marriage from the first date or, at the other extreme, a meaningless hookup. Part of that dynamic in reclaiming dating is to recognize what signs you are giving and what gestures you are revealing. Kisses and signs of physicality need to be held off until a deeper commitment has been made. Flowers and thoughtful gifts, however sweet and affirming, also need to be kept in proportion to the level of intimacy that the relationship has achieved. The setting of the date matters, too: walking on the beach by candlelight with dolphins trained to do flips in the background, for instance, might be best left for an engagement proposal and not the first date.

I've seen enough years go by at my school to witness a strange "last hurrah" effect when graduation approaches for the seniors. At the finale of their high school experience, the students seem to be most thoughtless about their intentions. At the edge of this major transition, many students start grasping at relationships or beginning romantic hookups "just for fun." Part of it is driven by loneliness, part of it could be mere lust, and part of it is an attempt to anchor themselves during an emotionally charged time in their lives. These relationships rarely end well, especially if both parties are about to go to different sides of the country for college in less than a month. Heartache seems to abound in these grasping moments when young people don't think through their actions, much less consider the self-centered desires that can infect the human heart.

Having the self-mastery not to engage in meaningless flirting or give misleading signs takes heroic effort. But I have seen it done, and the people who can respect others enough not to lure them into romance are learning how to love and put others first. It is not easy to do, and success does not come overnight. Sometimes it means embracing a lonely night or cutting short a conversation so that, out of love, we do not lead others on or promise them something that we cannot deliver. Real love is demanding and requires us to be faithful in connecting our actions to the words we're promising.

LIVE IT

Being aware of your intentions doesn't mean that you become a cold robot who shows zero affection on a date, but you will learn that restraint is a necessary human trait, whether it is in a professional workplace or in a romantic relationship. It starts with knowing what is going on within our heads and our hearts, curtailing any self-centered motives, and making sure our words and actions reflect authentic love.

Real love demands nothing less.

Bobby Angel is a campus minister and theology teacher at an all-boys' high school in California. He enjoys writing, surfing, and drinking too much coffee. He and his wife, Jackie, travel often and speak to youth and young adult audiences, sharing the gospel and the call to a life of chastity. They have three beautiful children who won't let them sleep.

LOOK AT ME, NOTICE ME
BY BETH SRI

"Look at me, notice me," uttered softly with a flip of the hair and a bat of the eye, was our high-school girls' joke.

But later in life, the phrase became a sort of challenge. I became what I would call now a "serial dater." I knew the drill: the rush of the initial crush, the flirting, the time "hanging out," which led to more ... but that wasn't enough. While progressing through these stages with one guy, at the same time I would be scoping out the next guy—a more intriguing, whole-package kind of guy. It always felt good to have someone interested in me. So, I'd leapfrog from relationship to relationship, from the "almost boyfriend" to the "next potential love interest."

Why the successive dating? Because, to borrow an expression from the character Cher in the movie *Clueless*, I was like "a full-on Monet [...] like a painting, see. From far away it's OK, but up close it's a big ol' mess." Yes, I wanted to be looked at, to be noticed, but at an arm's length—not up too close. I liked it when people noticed my cute outfit, pretty face, and flirtatious manner, but I didn't want anyone paying attention to what was behind that curtain ... inside and deep down.

The leapfrogging, if played correctly, could keep me afloat. If I just worked to keep it going, figuring out what it would take for me to snag that next great guy on the horizon, I would not sink. I would not have to look too hard at what was going on within. For if I did, I would see that being a serial dater was a way I could receive the external validation, attention, and praise that I craved. I was worth something then. Without someone to "work" towards attracting, I had only me. And what good was that? My own self-worth was virtually nonexistent.

It was easy to leave when things weren't as electric. Because that's when a real relationship could start. Reality would be set in motion. That's when I would panic. I was terrified of getting too close. If someone was on the doorstep of my heart, about to enter in, my intuition told me that he would not like what he would see. He would see I was a poser, "fake news," and worst of all I'd be rejected. So, better to move on to the next guy, get something going there, and hedge my bets, I thought.

Maybe it was because I was used to being on the move constantly, due to the back-and-forth visitation between my divorced parents. Or because their divorce set the tone: when a relationship doesn't work, it's best to leave. Yet, I was looking for a better life, for lasting happiness, for a better marriage than the broken one that brought me into this world. Maybe I was looking, hoping that one of these guys I dated could become my home, in a sense. My security blanket, my savior. But no one felt safe enough to let them see the big ol' Monet mess up close.

The thrill of the chase eventually took its toll on me. My heart was like a rubber band stretched one too many times that snapped back on me with its full force, with a loud snap, a painful sting, and a red mark to prove it. I had had to work hard to get each new guy interested in me and then work hard to keep him interested. Then I had to work hard again to hide certain parts of me, lest I be discovered for a fraud. It was a lot of hard work. I was tired. I'd had enough. It was time to retire my serial dater status.

While getting out of the serial dating hamster wheel was liberating, I had no idea what to expect. What was my life supposed to look like now? How would I spend my Saturday nights? Would anyone even want to hang out with me on the weekends?

At this point in my life, I discovered the treasure of good friends. In time, I found like-minded individuals—just a few, really—who shared similar interests, similar values. Through our time just being together, at lunch, on Saturday nights, over holiday breaks, they grew into real friends. I learned how friendship worked, the give and take of sharing life together. I began to trust them. It was here that I began to slowly prop open the door of my heart. Over time, they saw glimmers of my "big ol' mess" inside . . . and they didn't run away.

Eventually I returned to the dating scene, changed. Dating meant something. I didn't take it lightly. The young men around me were not something to be used or to be played. They were not landing pads to make me feel better about myself. Most of all, I didn't just want to be looked at and noticed. I wanted to be known.

Beth Sri is a writer, wife, and mother who served as one of the first FOCUS missionaries and has mentored young adult women for twenty years. Her website, borntodothis.org, encourages women in their call to marriage and motherhood. She has a passion for Jane Austen, distance running, and dark chocolate and is married to Dr. Edward Sri.

GUYS, HERE'S HOW TO ASK A GIRL ON A DATE
BY KEVIN COTTER

During my senior year in high school, I became friends with Rebecca (not her real name). At first, we just began to talk more, but we quickly found ways to hang out all the time. It was pretty obvious that there was an attraction between us, but I was a senior and she was a sophomore. I knew that I would be heading off to college soon, and I was not quite sure how I felt about a long-distance relationship. I had a choice to make: either date Rebecca despite the distance or scale back our relationship to a normal level of friendship.

So which did I choose? I chose to ... well, not make a choice. Instead, Rebecca and I began a confusing three-year cycle of relationship ambiguity. I would often say that we were just friends, but my friends, who saw right through me, called her "my pseudo"—short for pseudo-girlfriend. At the end of the three years, I "broke up" with Rebecca, even though we were not officially dating. Think about that for a moment...

SACRIFICE

Dating and marriage are amazing things, but at the root of love is sacrifice. Think about any great relationship that you have witnessed, whether in real life or the movies. There is always an element of great sacrifice involved.

And yet, our culture tries to offer us love without sacrifice. Many times, men follow this lie and fail to commit to a woman. Why? Because we do not want to risk rejection. We would rather just go with the flow and see what happens. This is what I did with Rebecca; this is what boys do. But men step up and are willing to sacrifice their reputations and hearts rather than make women suffer in ambiguity.

MY CHALLENGE

My challenge to guys reading this: Choose to act like a man. Fortunately, I didn't make the same mistake when I asked my wife, Lisa, out for the first time. Whether you have never asked a girl out before or have made my same mistake several times, here are some tips on how to ask a woman out like a man.

STEP 1: ASK HER IN PERSON—DON'T TEXT

Lately, a number of women have told me that they are frequently asked out by guys via text. This is lame and unmanly. There's no risk involved, it's impersonal, and it does not honor the woman. If you can't ask face to face, don't ask. If you can't see her face to face, then call her. But DON'T TEXT!

STEP 2: TELL HER WHY YOU ARE ASKING

It's helpful to give a little context for your request. You might mention that the time you have spent together helped you realize certain characteristics about her. Some things to look out for here: First, don't be shallow. Be sincere—but don't go too deep. No need to tell her all of your dreams for your future together or how you think she is the one you'll marry. Just give her a few compliments and a bit of a story so she knows you aren't coming out of nowhere.

STEP 3: TELL HER WHAT YOU ARE ASKING

There are many different types of dating. Perhaps you don't know her very well and want to take her on a date to get to know her better. Possibly you have been friends for a while and want to start dating on a regular basis.

No matter what, make sure you articulate what it is you are asking her. One of the worst feelings for a woman is to know that a guy likes her but then be confused about what that means. Give her an easy story she can tell her friends and family.

STEP 4: HAVE A PLAN

Whether you are asking her on one date or asking her to date seriously, have a plan. For instance: "I'd like to take you to dinner this Friday night at 7. Are you free?"

Don't ask her out and then ask, "What do you want to do?" If you want to make sure the date goes well, then take the time to ask her or her friends what she likes to eat. And feel free to plan something beyond a meal by planning an activity or two. It doesn't have to be amazing, it just has to be thought through.

WORTH THE RISK

Asking someone out on a date this way is hard. There is risk involved, and that can be scary. What if she says no? I know the feeling. When I asked my wife out for the first time, I knew I would be seeing her a lot in the near future: We were already signed up to run a marathon together! Can you imagine running for four hours with someone who turned you down?

But I promise you: It's worth it! First, show honor to whomever you are asking. Second, even if she turns you down, you now have a great reputation. Other girls will think, wow, I wish a guy would ask me out like that!

Good luck!

Kevin Cotter serves FOCUS as the Senior Director of Curriculum. He is the author of numerous resources and books, including *Dating Detox: 40 Days of Perfecting Love in an Imperfect World* with his wife Lisa. *Dating Detox* helps you formulate a concrete plan so that you gain the freedom to love and be loved. Featuring daily chapters filled with stories, teachings, and resolutions, this forty-day detox provides a practical "cleanse" for those who want to purify themselves from the poisoned dating culture and live a life of authentic freedom.

DATING WITH DETACHMENT
BY JACKIE FRANCOIS ANGEL

One of the most difficult aspects of dating intentionally is learning how to be detached. You may hear the word "detached" and think "cold" or "stand-offish," but in a dating scenario, it really means that you are content regardless of the outcome—whether your date is meant to marry you *or* someone else. Detachment helps make the journey of dating something to appreciate and not resent. It is the basis for healthy, mature relationships that are counter-cultural, different from the dysfunctional relationships in reality TV and books.

For many people, a date often brings over-attachment. When dating, we quickly get attached to each other physically, emotionally, intellectually, or spiritually. This happens because we treat the other as if we were already exclusively committed. This over-attachment can blind us to the reality of the other person. We overemphasize strengths, shrug off faults, or make excuses for weaknesses. In the end, we fall more in love with the "romance" of the relationship than the actual person. When we finally do awaken to the reality of the person, we can be disillusioned, heart-broken, and bitter.

But dating doesn't have to be full of hurt and disappointment like a Taylor Swift song. We don't have to end up hating someone's guts or "ghosting" them by disappearing off the face of the earth. How to avoid the hurt? Be detached. Imagine being asked out and realizing ten minutes into the evening that your date is "trouble." If you are detached, you can have a good time on one date but realize this just isn't the right person for you. On the other hand, if you are not detached, you risk getting stuck. You would keep dating, and within a few dates you would find yourself physically intimate, emotionally divulging your whole life story, and maybe even allowing the other person to treat you like a "savior." With detachment, you could walk away after one date, and no one would get hurt.

Being detached is the key to the new way of dating in *The Dating Project*. It means getting to know someone amiably but having the maturity to make a choice. If you realize the other is not the right person for you, stop dating. Don't lead them on. But if your date *is* the right kind of person for you, intentionally pursue him or her in an exclusive relationship.

Detachment also means having the confidence to be a happy single person who knows that no other person will ever satisfy every desire of your heart. This self-confidence will allow you to be a person who is life-giving in a relationship rather than life-sucking.

So you may be wondering, "What are some ways to stay detached?" Here are a few guidelines for happy, detached dating:

1. HAVE BOUNDARIES

The Dating Project mentions quite a few good boundaries: for instance, no alcohol on the dates, keep the first date less than ninety minutes, don't spend a lot of money. But here are some others that may help you stay detached:

Physical boundaries: The first stage of dating, when you may be going on multiple nonexclusive dates with different people, is about getting to know someone better. It is not about a hookup or going as "far" as your date will let you. You should only physically do things that you could do with all those other dates watching you. In clear terms, treat your date as you would your brother or sister. Your intimacy level should match your commitment level. It is not until you are in an exclusive relationship that the romantic, physical signs of affection should come into play. And even then, you aren't married 'til you're married. Do not act like a married couple physically until you have made a life-long commitment to that person in marriage. Keep the affection simple and pure.

Emotional boundaries: It's very easy to over-attach emotionally when you are dating. You may daydream or fantasize about the other person until you build him or her up in your head and heart. But this means you are falling in love with the idea of the person instead of the real person. The first stage of a dating relationship is about getting to know the reality of the person—his or her interests, likes and dislikes, personality and disposition. Remember, too, that dating is not meant to look like a therapy session, where you spill all your heart's greatest desires and fears. Initial dates are not the place to tell your family's problems, nor a place to complain about your life, nor a place to emotionally manipulate someone to believe you are way better than you are. (Well, there's no place for that!) Emotional boundaries come from emotional maturity. Reality TV presents people behaving like toddlers in relationships: throwing tantrums, whining, being needy. This is dysfunctional, not normal or healthy. Be honest. Be yourself. Be confident. Have fun! Be an emotionally mature person on your own, and you will be an emotionally mature person on a date!

Intellectual boundaries: How do you over-attach yourself intellectually? Well, say for instance you are both Star Wars nerds. If you find this out on the first date, it might make you think "this is the one" just because you both know every character and planet in every film. However, if Star Wars dominates all your conversations, it could be a crutch. It could be a way to avoid talking about other things that you don't agree on. So stay detached! Another way you might over-attach intellectually is if you fall in love with someone's status or degree or brain. Just because your date is the World Spelling Bee Champ doesn't automatically make him or her "the one" for you, even if you have dreamed about marrying a smart person your whole life. Get to know someone in all his or her different facets before attaching yourself.

Spiritual boundaries: It is tempting to think that sharing the same religion makes you an automatic match with your date. But dig deeper. "Well, he's Christian" could mean that he goes to church only on Christmas and Easter, or it could mean that he is getting his Ph.D. in Theology. Dating is about learning the nuances of a person, even in their spirituality, and seeing if you are on the same page. So don't idealize someone just because he or she is Christian. Or agnostic. Or an atheist. Find out more about your date and see if you are truly on the same page.

2. REMEMBER THAT EVERY PERSON YOU GO ON A DATE WITH IS SOMEONE'S FUTURE WIFE OR HUSBAND

This may help you treat him or her with a greater respect and care for body, heart, mind, and soul. If you had to tell your dates' future spouses everything you did with them, for them, or to them, would you be proud or ashamed?

3. HAVE A GAME PLAN

Remember that your time is precious and so is your date's. If you find out within a date or two that this person is just not right for you, have the courtesy (and courage) not to lead him or her on. If that person asks you on another date, charitably decline. If you were the initial pursuer and do not see this relationship becoming exclusive, let the other person know. The rejection will sting, but people will *always* be glad you were honest instead of leading them on and wasting their time. All the time you stay in the wrong dating relationship is time you are wasting not being in the right one.

4. THE BIGGEST KEY TO DETACHMENT IS BEING A CONFIDENT, WHOLE, AND HEALTHY PERSON

If you are not single and happy, you definitely won't be married and happy. Nor will you be dating and happy. If you are insecure as a single person, you will suck the life out of any person you date. If you have issues (like depression or anxiety or past abuse), get help from a therapist to become healthy emotionally and physically. Therapy is not a sign of weakness. In fact, your future dates—and eventually your future spouse—will be glad that you are a whole person on your own. They will be glad they don't have to be your "savior" or "fix" you. The healthier you are as an individual, the better you will be as a dating person, and the easier it will be to have healthy detachment.

Detachment is difficult, but it is essential for a healthy dating experience. You may regret being over-attached in past relationships, but you will never regret having integrity and healthy detachment in your future relationships!

Jackie Francois Angel is an international speaker, worship leader, and author from Orange County, California. In 2013, she married the love of her life, Bobby Angel, and together they travel, speak about the love of God, and attempt to raise three rambunctious saints. They are the authors of the marriage devotional *Forever*.

GOING FROM "FRIENDS" TO "MORE THAN FRIENDS"
ANDREW SWAFFORD

"But I don't want to ruin our friendship."

What do you do when you like someone but don't want to "jeopardize" your friendship?

Well, the answer is not to hang out, flirt for the next year, and develop a strong emotional attachment along the way, with no commitment from either side—only to lead to jealousy and confusion when a third party enters the scene.

How do we avoid this trap?

If you have gotten to know someone well as a friend—and he or she is the kind of person you'd like to end up with some day—then take the risk and move forward. Especially in groups gathered in religious settings, I've seen quite a bit of stalling here. In other words, the men and women in these groups have rejected the hookup culture and are striving to follow God, but they are often shy about showing romantic interest. And, unfortunately, relationships that would otherwise blossom never get off the ground. Right here is where I frequently hear the line, "I don't want to ruin our friendship."

But more often than not, it's a friendship in motion—that is, you are probably not destined to remain "just friends" forever. Your friendship will probably change as life continues and one of you gets married, for example. So, if you have a good friend that you greatly admire and respect, and you would like to pursue the possibility of a future with that friend, take the risk.

To use a cheesy but helpful phrase, there need to be two DTRs (defining the relationship). First, there is the initial showing of interest—something as simple as "I really appreciate our friendship. I'd like to get to know you better." If someone says this to you, then you're not *just* friends. After a period of time (there is no magic length, but it's best not to extend it any longer than necessary—I'm thinking a month or two), there needs to be an end to this "getting to know you better" phase. And so we proceed to the second DTR: the "what are we?" conversation. At this point, we either make a commitment, or we return to being just friends. The "getting to know you better" phase ends. (For more here, see Sarah Swafford's book *Emotional Virtue* in the recommended resources section at the end of this guide).

If we are not going to make a commitment, we can still be friends, but we are no longer "friends in motion." That is, we are no longer pursuing the possibility of a relationship together. At this point, we need to return to the "just friends" category. A good test for "just friends" is this: would I engage in these same activities and conversations with this person if I were seriously dating someone else?

The twofold DTR (initial showing of interest and then making a commitment) has the advantage of taking some of the pressure off the first phase. Especially in the spiritual communities I've seen, very often nobody is dating—in part, because asking someone on a date becomes so monumental that it feels like a marriage proposal. This, it seems to me, is an overreaction against the hookup culture—a good reaction, but perhaps swinging the pendulum too far. If the first DTR is simply the initial showing of interest, hopefully it becomes a little less intimidating. At the second DTR, the relationship obviously becomes more serious—or at least has the potential to become so.

Now what if someone pursues the first DTR (initial showing of interest) with you and you don't feel the same way? Just politely say, "I appreciate your friendship, but I see us as just friends." And if someone says that to you, take the hint. It might sting a bit, but at least there's clarity.

What if you're thinking—"I'm a girl, shouldn't I wait for the guy to ask me out?" Ideally, yes, of course. But we don't live in an ideal world. For my part, there are all kinds of healthy ways a girl can drop hints and show interest (like consistently laughing at a guy's dumb jokes). We guys are dense, but not that dense. If you drop these hints and there is no reaction, simply move on; a guy who does not follow up on these hints probably just isn't interested.

Yes, the man should take initiative and show leadership here; but, for my part, far worse is the ongoing confusion and gray area. If female-initiated hints lead to clarity sooner, then all the better.

Also, pursue even the first DTR with only one person at a time. This better communicates sincerity and interest and will minimize unhealthy aspects of the gray area.

Finally, don't date just for fun; you want to be confident that each person you date is the *kind* of person you would like to end up with. And the litmus test is this: If something happened to me, would I trust this person with my kids someday—as their primary influence?

Since the second DTR does move into a semi-serious phase—after all, you are acknowledging that this person is the kind of person you would like to end up with—wait until you are ready to marry. Dating in this kind of a committed way doesn't make sense if marriage is a decade away. In other words, exclusively committed and emotionally attached relationships in high school seldom go well for a couple of reasons. First, there is so much growth happening at that time that you often miss out on the opportunity to grow with friends and really grow spiritually. Focusing on friends and spiritual growth in high school helps you become the person God has called you to be (not the person that fits the mold and expectations of your significant other over the past two years). Second, it is exceedingly difficult—just as a matter of basic biology and psychology—for a couple to get very close emotionally and expect to remain pure sexually for the next ten years. Persevering in chastity would be difficult enough in high school, let alone throughout four more years of college. And remember, anything that aims at the arousal of the other person crosses a line that is reserved for marriage.

My advice: Run to Jesus. Make great friends with both men and women. And when the time is right and someone has the character to pique your interest, then take the risk—at least with the first DTR. You never know where it might end up. But if you don't even try, you already know the answer.

Andrew Swafford is Associate Professor of Theology at Benedictine College. He holds a doctorate in sacred theology and is the author of *Spiritual Survival in the Modern World*, *John Paul II to Aristotle and Back Again*, and *Nature and Grace*. He lives with his wife, Sarah, and their four children in Atchison, Kansas.

THE WORST THING SHE COULD SAY IS NO
BY PAUL J. KIM

It's happened to most of us guys. You're at a party. You see this gorgeous girl from across the room. She's perfect. And then the frantic inner dialogue begins in your mind:

"Should I go talk to her?

Nah, you're crazy, she's way out of your league.

What if she already has a boyfriend?

Of course she already has a boyfriend, she's a model! Why the heck would she want to talk to you anyway?

Well, sometimes really pretty girls have a thing for ugly guys, and even skinny guys.

That's because those guys are filthy rich and are CEOs of startup companies. Too bad all that you have in your checking account is debt. If you decide to go on the suicide mission and actually go talk to her, she's going to give you a look of disgust and laugh because you're just not her type. Then all of her friends are going to laugh at you in slow motion. Besides, you have nothing interesting to say to her! Don't be a jerk and waste her time."

The girl then actually looks your way, smiles, and you respond by quickly darting your eyes away from her, ordering a drink, and cowering off into some corner where you're safe from any amount of social risk.

Where did I gather all this insight in regard to this sort of inner dialogue, which, I believe, universally afflicts young men all throughout the world? From my memory. Because I've been guilty of it, too. So. Many. Times. And if I'm honest with myself, there were a number of things at play in my inability to act with confidence, courage, and class in moments such as those. But one of the primary reasons had to do with my fear of rejection.

Men, what is the worst thing that the girl in that scenario could have said if you walked up, had a conversation with her, and asked her out sometime? "No." Perhaps even, "No *thanks."* And then what would have happened? You would have shrieked as your body began to shrink into the size of a plastic figurine, right? Wrong. If a girl declines your offer to go out on a date or refuses to give you her number, that's OK. There are billions of other women in the world, and you've just narrowed down the search for your future spouse.

In my experience as a marriage and family therapist, one of the methods I would use in my counseling sessions with clients who came in with phobias or anxiety was an intervention method called exposure therapy. As the name entails, the technique involved exposing the client to the very thing that they were afraid of, in a controlled environment, repeatedly. Often times, these fears were highly irrational and involved categories such as the fear of balloons, elevators, or not having access to hand sanitizer every few minutes.

Naturally, the client would be filled with anxious thoughts and feelings as they encountered their worst nightmares. But little by little, over the course of a number of sessions, they came to grasp that much of the fear was based on a false meaning that they had placed on the object, setting, or circumstance. It was rewarding to witness the weight being lifted off their shoulders as they learned to overcome their fears, replace irrational thoughts with truth, and prove to themselves that they could be free of these manufactured shackles in their minds.

The reason I bring this up is because I believe that the fear of rejection, or social anxiety, can be overcome in just the same way. It's going to involve some initial exposure to discomfort and fear, but you'll be fine. Here is your first mission, if you choose to accept it:

Pick a day this week where you can walk up to a woman during the day in public, such as at a mall, and start a conversation. Ask her an interesting opening question like,

"Hello, sorry to bother you, but could I get your honest opinion, as a woman, about what I could get for my mom (or sister depending on whose birthday is coming up sooner) that would make her feel special on her birthday?"

You'll probably feel nervous and awkward asking, but keep your cool. Don't breathe heavily or stare at her with your eyes wide open like a crazy person. Focus on being casual, relaxed, and knowing that you're not going to die. You will be pleasantly surprised at the number of women who might be taken aback at first but are willing to help you with such a thoughtful question that has to do with treating the first woman in your life with love and consideration. This is a trait that any woman would appreciate.

As she gives her response and seeks to help you out, follow up by thanking her, and then introduce your name. Then ask what her name is. Then give her a compliment. Remember, the purpose of this exercise is not to be manipulative, creepy, or some raging pick-up artist. Rather, it is for you to overcome your fear of approaching a woman you don't know (or don't know well) and be able to carry on a conversation.

If the conversation continues, then great! Go with the flow and show her that you not only know how to lead a conversation, but you are a man with substance, intelligence, class, and charm.

"But what if I don't have substance, intelligence, class, or charm? Or I don't know the art of conversation??"

Well, my friend, that's where you need to continue developing yourself into a man who possesses such qualities. Read, study, grow, exercise, serve, travel, pray, seek to grow in your Faith, and expose yourself to things (good things) outside of your comfort zone that challenge you to level up. You have what it takes. You have something to offer. Show her that you are a man who has goals, direction, and a passion for life.

If, at the end of this conversation, you feel like you would like to get to know her more and take her out on a date, then be direct and ask her:

"Hey, it's been really nice talking to you, and I'd love to get to know you more. Could I take you out for coffee or lunch sometime?"

If she says, "*Sure,*" then take out your phone and ask for her number, not her Facebook, Instagram, or Snapchat account. Please. That's a cop out.

If she says, "*Uhhh, no thanks,*" or "*Sorry, I have a boyfriend,*" then remain calm and respond by saying,

"*No worries, I appreciate you helping me out. Have a great rest of your day.*"

Walk away and don't be weird about it, cry, or kick an inanimate object. Know that this is not a failure but, rather, a success. You have grown in your confidence and ability to put yourself out there. Congratulations. It doesn't mean you are an unlovable freak who will be forever alone; it just means that she was not compatible with you. Carry on, brother, there are many more fish in the sea. And the more you engage in this type of exercise, the more you will learn to be the best version of yourself in social settings.

Ultimately, women appreciate a guy's boldness and confidence in asking them out. I have a friend who was not even attracted to her fiancé when they first met, but she honored the fact that he was direct and that he took the risk of initiating. Fast forward years later, and now they're engaged to be married. Boom.

I know another guy who, nearly five years ago, attended his friend's wedding without a date, as usual. As he looked around the reception hall, he saw this beautiful girl with a stunning smile. Normally he would have shied away from approaching a complete stranger, but instead he decided to take a risk. He introduced himself, asked her an interesting question like, *"Tell me the meaning behind the tattoo on your shoulder,"* and the night continued with conversation, laughter, dancing, and the crucial phone number exchange.

That guy was me, the gorgeous girl with the tattoo is now my wife, and I'm currently writing this article on our kitchen table as she dances across the room, making our two beautiful kids laugh. I'm so grateful I overcame my fear and took a risk that day. I'll be rooting for you as you go and take yours.

Paul J. Kim is one of the most sought-after faith-based youth speakers in America. He has presented in nearly all fifty states and several countries, utilizing music (beatboxing), comedy, and inspirational talks. He has released two music albums, his videos on YouTube have accumulated over a million views, and he presents to over 30,000 people each year at events throughout the world. In his free time, Paul enjoys long walks on the beach, surfing, talking to strangers in random accents, and pointing out God's sense of humor. He lives in southern California with his beautiful wife and two children. pjkmusic.com

DEALING WITH REJECTION
BY JACINTA FLORENCE

Nobody likes rejection. When it happens, the feeling that comes stings like a jellyfish (although I've never been stung by a jellyfish). I was recently interested in a guy and spent a lot of one-on-one time with him. I felt the need to let him know that I was interested in him, even though I knew that I might be rejected. What happened after that was quite comical, in my opinion. He told me that he had no attraction to me whatsoever. My response: "Tell me how you really feel." I was humbled, for sure. And I knew I might have lost a friend—*for now*.

I recently heard someone say that you should not let the fear of ruining a friendship hold you back from your future. I took her advice, and I must say that it is solid. I may have lost a friend *for now*, but I've gained so much. Think about it: What if I held back my attractions for this guy and continued to spend one-on-one time with him for months, not knowing if he was interested? Now that I know his thoughts about me, I have moved on with my life. That time that I would formerly be spending with him, I am spending cultivating great friendships with other awesome people whom I admire.

However, because rejection can still sting, I've put together five tips for how to deal with it:

Laugh: Laughing may or may not be my love language. When rejection or other disappointments come up in life, finding humor in the situation makes it a lot easier to get through.

Love even when you feel unloved: Love always desires the greatest good for the beloved. That definition of love can be tested in the face of rejection. Instead of feeling sorry for yourself or tearing down the other person, use rejection as an invitation to love in the truest sense. How? One way would be to pray for the person who rejected you, that he or she would find the right person. Also, get involved in works of service for others. You have gifts, and the world needs your love.

Move on with your life: Now that you have a clear answer that the person is not interested, use this as an opportunity to move on. That door has closed for a reason.

Form yourself: Don't be passive in waiting for love to "happen" to you. Take some time to read some of the resources at the end of this booklet.

Live your life: As an almost-thirty-year-old single woman, I would say: enjoy the single years! I spent most of high school and my early twenties constantly in a relationship. Now that I am single, I'm using this time to the full. Do things that you love. Travel, write a blog, learn an instrument, and build virtuous friendships. Live now, and the guy or girl will come when the time is right. In your pursuit to find your vocation, do not let rejection hold you back from continuing to seek authentic love.

Jacinta Florence hails from Tulsa, Oklahoma, and is a graduate of St. Gregory's University. As a young adult, she had a profound experience of leaving a lifestyle immersed in the culture to embrace her Faith. Her experience of working with Generation Life as a missionary led her to the Augustine Institute where she is getting her master's in theology. Jacinta now resides in Denver, Colorado. When she's not studying in a coffee shop, she enjoys road trips and traveling to new states.

WHY I DON'T DATE MEN WHO ARE "WILLING" TO SAVE SEX
BY ARLEEN SPENCELEY

"There's something I need to tell you," I said to a man on his couch in a Tampa apartment. He—then in his late twenties and interested in me—nodded and waited for me to say it. I—then in my early twenties—breathed in before I spoke: "I'm saving sex for marriage."

That's because I practice the virtue of chastity—a decision we make every day to do the right thing regarding sex, which I believe was designed for married couples. Since I'm not married, the right thing for me involves abstaining from it.
I breathed out while he silently processed what I had said. Then he turned his face toward mine and spoke: "If you want to wait, I'm willing." But waiting had never been part of his world. He agreed to abstain from sex with me because he knew that if he didn't, I wouldn't date him. He agreed to

behave *as if* he practiced chastity, but he was only bound to abstinence by my prohibition of nonmarital sex.

He respected my boundary, until he didn't—until he mocked my decision to save sex and chalked it up to "immaturity" in an effort to manipulate me into changing my mind. He said "no guy will wait that long," and he begged me to break my promise to practice chastity. Instead, I broke up with him.

I learned a lot in that relationship, including this: I would never date a guy again who was only "willing" to save sex.

BECAUSE I DON'T WANT A MAN WHO ACTS CHASTELY; I WANT A MAN WHO IS CHASTE

Chaste people (meaning those who strive to practice chastity) have apprenticeships in self-mastery. We resolve to govern our appetites instead of being governed by them. A man who is "willing" to save sex in order to date me is not a man who governs his appetites. He is a man who makes chaste girlfriends do that for him. If I date him, I govern two sets of appetites, which makes me an enabler: he doesn't have to practice self-mastery if *I* master him.

BECAUSE A MAN WHO DOESN'T PRACTICE CHASTITY DOESN'T DEFINE SEX THE SAME WAY I DO

We who practice chastity believe sex is a sacred, physical sign of the commitment spouses made to each other when they were married. It is an expression of their unity, fundamentally designed to bond them and to make babies. A man who is "willing" to save sex—but would have nonmarital sex if he had my permission—by default does not define sex the way I do. How can we be united by sex in marriage if we can't agree on the purpose of sex?

BECAUSE A MAN WHO WOULD FORSAKE VIRTUE (HIS *OR* MINE) IF ONLY I GAVE HIM PERMISSION IS A MAN WHOSE STANDARDS ARE TOO LOW

A man who is "willing" to save sex is a man whose choice to abstain from nonmarital sex likely is not underlaid by much other than the absence of my consent. He would be just as content—or more content—dating a woman who does not practice chastity. But I do not want to marry a man who settles for a chaste woman. I want a man who *wants* a chaste woman, who holds a high bar for me because he wants me to become the woman God designed me to be.

BECAUSE MEN ARE CAPABLE OF MORE THAN THE WORLD AROUND THEM SAYS THEY ARE

"No guy will wait that long" is a lie, and boys who are taught that turn into men who believe it. But I hold up a higher bar than that for men because I think my future kids deserve a dad who can reach it, because I believe men *can* reach it, because I believe God created them able to do it.

But my decision not to date them if they are only "willing" to save sex doesn't sit well with some people.

One person once said that "by automatically avoiding these men, you rule out the ... opportunity to aid in someone's conversion."

Another said, "I would not automatically disqualify someone if they were ["willing" to wait]. Not every guy received good formation, often through no fault of his own."

Still another said a guy's "willingness is a step in the right direction and is worthy of great respect!"

And I get it. An unchaste man's decision to abstain from sex is indicative of his potential to change. And indeed, a decision to date a man who does not believe what I do—about sex or about anything at all—could be a catalyst for his becoming the kind of guy I want him to be. Sure, I would like for a catalyst to exist. I would like for him to become the best he can be, no matter who he is, which includes having the interest in governing himself and the ability to do it. If an unchaste man knew what I know, he would *want* to practice chastity. And yes, he could learn if I date him. But I, now in my early thirties, *still* won't.

BECAUSE CHASTE PEOPLE DON'T OWE UNCHASTE PEOPLE A CHANCE

Neither my attraction to an unchaste man nor an unchaste man's potential to change obligates me to date him, because nothing obligates any person to date another. It is your right to have a stable set of standards, and it is your right to rule out the people who don't meet them.

BECAUSE PEOPLE WHO PRACTICE CHASTITY *DO* EXIST

Is a chaste person actually hesitant to rule out an unchaste person because he or she can be the catalyst for his or her conversion, or is it because he or she is afraid that people who are already chaste don't exist? But people who currently practice chastity—regardless of their pasts—*do* exist. And I don't meet them while I'm dating a man who is not chaste.

AND BECAUSE A ROMANTIC RELATIONSHIP WITH A CHASTE PERSON IS NOT AN UNCHASTE PERSON'S ONLY PATH TO CHASTITY

Any unchaste man I meet *does* need an introduction to chastity. But I do not need to be his girlfriend in order for him to receive an introduction. A chaste person's decision not to date an unchaste person does not deprive an unchaste person of what he or she actually needs. If we treat unchaste people like they cannot become chaste unless a chaste person dates them, we underestimate them—and we underestimate God.

Arleen Spenceley is author of the book *Chastity Is for Lovers: Single, Happy, and (Still) a Virgin*. She works as a staff writer for the *Tampa Bay Times*. She has a bachelor's degree in journalism and a master's degree in counseling, both from the University of South Florida. She blogs at arleenspenceley.com.

FOUR HELPFUL RULES FOR DISCERNMENT
FATHER MIKE SCHMITZ

When it comes to making big decisions, we're often anxious. We often end up saying, "God, you tell me what to do."

That is not a bad thing. It's good because it means we are telling God, "I want your will more than I want my will." When it comes to whom to date or when to marry, I want God to tell me and I'll do it.

It is a good thing to want to do God's will. That's why we pray, "Thy will be done." It is core to being a saint. In fact, as C.S. Lewis put it, the saint is the person who says, "God, thy will be done," while the person in hell is the one to whom God says, "Your will be done." But I remember reading an author who said that when it comes to figuring out God's will in our lives, we are often hoping to evade responsibility. Often, we don't necessarily want to do God's will as much as we want relief from the responsibility of having to make a decision for ourselves. Many times, what God is counting on us to do is make the decision ourselves. Unless God steps into our lives in a direct way and says, "This is what I want you to do," it seems like he often says, "OK, just choose."

God has given us a great deal of freedom. He has blessed us with wisdom and intelligence. He has given us a will, and he wants us to use the intellect and the will when it comes to big decisions. So how do we do that?

Ask yourself four questions. Think of them as asking four questions about a door.

The first question about a decision I have to make is this: **Is this a good door?** In other words, is this something that God has said never to do? Has he said never open this door? If it's a good door or even a neutral door, then it is a possibility. If it's a bad door, then the door is off-limits. It's locked. I do not need to go in there. If God has revealed something, it is clear. So if someone is wondering, "Should I cheat on my wife or not?", the answer is no. God said not to do that, so don't do that. That's clear enough. The answer is also clear if God has placed a truth as a conviction on your heart.

If this is a good door, then I ask the second question: **Is this an open door?** Is this an actual thing I could do? Is this a possibility or reality for me? For example, I do not have to discern whether I should try out for the NBA or not. That, for me, is a closed door. It's a fine door, but I don't have to bang against this door, because it is closed to me. Or, suppose you asked someone out on a date, and he or she responded with a "no, thanks." This means that at least right now dating that person is a closed door. You don't have to continue to bang against that door.

The third question is this: **Is this a wise door?** Now here things get a little complicated, and you need to start thinking more. Knowing where you have been, knowing who you are right now, and also knowing who you want to be—who you believe God is calling you to be—would this be a wise door for you to open? Would this be a wise door for you to walk through? Would this be a wise decision in your life? You ask yourself this question because you know yourself. You know the kind of person you are. You know your struggles, you know your strengths, and you know the kind of person you want to be. So, knowing all those things, would this be a wise door for you to walk through?

Often, people say, "Well, I just have to choose this." Not necessarily. Ask yourself the questions. Is this a good door? Is this an open door? Is this a wise door? Would this be good for you to go through? Think about a relationship. You might already know enough about this person to know that it would not be a good idea for you to pursue a relationship with him or her. Maybe it's good. Maybe it's open—the other person is interested. But it wouldn't be wise, right? It wouldn't actually get you to where you want to go. It wouldn't necessarily help the other person to get to where he or she wants to go. If that were true, the relationship would not be a wise door.

The fourth question is one that people hate when I bring up. But it is a real question. The fourth question is this: If this is a good door, an open door, a wise door, then **is this a door that I want?** Why ask this question? Because if God has not revealed yet that you should not go through this door or you should go through this door, then you actually get to choose. Is this the door I actually want to go through? Is this a decision I want to make?

God has given us so much freedom. He has given us freedom to use our minds and to use our wills. I believe he often says, "Any of these choices are choices you can make. I will be there on the other side." So you may be asking, "Should I marry this person or that person?" OK, well, is this good? Open? Wise? And a door you want? Is this a person you'd like to marry? "But what about that person?" Well, who do you want? "Should I date this person or that person?" Well, are they open, available to you? Are they wise, knowing yourself? And which one is the one you desire?

Why ask these questions? Because we can't just keep dismissing and putting choices off on God. We have to actually make decisions and take responsibility. One of the marks of adulthood is taking responsibility for oneself, for one's decisions.

So, when you have to make a dating decision, take responsibility. And even if you make the wrong decision after asking all those questions, the Lord will still be with you. He always provides a way to get back on track.

Father Mike Schmitz is a Catholic priest, author, and speaker in the Diocese of Duluth, Minnesota. Working with Ascension, he is the author of the *Belonging* study program and is featured in *Altaration* and *I Will Follow*. His weekly YouTube videos available through Ascension's outlet, Ascension Presents, continue to grow in popularity as do his homilies, also available online. He currently runs the Newman Center at the University of Minnesota-Duluth and is the Director of Youth and Young Adult Ministry for the diocese.

THE
DATING
ASSIGNMENT

HERE ARE THE RULES:

1. ASK IN-PERSON
No text messages. No Facebook. No Snapchat. No Instagram. Face to face. Eye to eye. IRL.

2. WITHIN THREE DAYS
Waiting longer creates unnecessary anxiety, invites drama, and sets the stage for unsolicited (or worse, solicited) opinions and advice.

3. A ROMANTIC INTEREST
Pick someone that catches your eye. A romantic interest. Think possible, not soulmate.

4. SOMEBODY NEW
This should not be a date with a person whom you've dated before.

5. BE OPEN & HONEST
Avoid the dreaded "acci-date." While you do not have to use the word "date," make sure you're clear this is a date.

6. ONLY 45-90 MINS
Leave 'em wanting more—and give yourself a hard out if you don't find yourself wanting more.

7. MAKE A PLAN
No "So…what do you want to do?" Take initiative to plan the date. Show you respect their time.

8. YOU ASK, YOU PAY
Make it clear: This person is worth the money—and you're worth the investment, too.

9. BUT ONLY $10
You're not a spendthrift, but, geez, you're not royalty, either. Unless you are. Then still $10.

10. NO TOUCHY
How far is too far? An "A-frame" hug at the end of the date is far enough.

11. TELL THREE PEOPLE
Cold feet happen, but it's less likely if you've got support. Only three teammates, though; TMZ is everywhere!

12. GO ALONE
You've got support, but for the love of Pete, no wingman, best friend, or group dates.

DATING JOURNAL

WHO AM I GOING TO ASK OUT?

HOW DID THE ASKING GO?

WHEN/WHERE IS THE DATE?

HOW DID THE DATE GO?

DO I WANT THERE TO BE A SECOND DATE?

IF SO, WHAT WILL I DO ABOUT IT?

HOW DID THE SECOND DATE GO?

DATING JOURNAL

WHO AM I GOING TO ASK OUT?

HOW DID THE ASKING GO?

WHEN/WHERE IS THE DATE?

HOW DID THE DATE GO?

DO I WANT THERE TO BE A SECOND DATE?

IF SO, WHAT WILL I DO ABOUT IT?

HOW DID THE SECOND DATE GO?

DATING JOURNAL

WHO AM I GOING TO ASK OUT?

_____

_____

HOW DID THE ASKING GO?

_____

_____

_____

_____

WHEN/WHERE IS THE DATE?

_____

_____

HOW DID THE DATE GO?

_____

_____

_____

_____

_____

_____

DO I WANT THERE TO BE A SECOND DATE?

IF SO, WHAT WILL I DO ABOUT IT?

HOW DID THE SECOND DATE GO?

DATING JOURNAL

WHO AM I GOING TO ASK OUT?

_____
_____

HOW DID THE ASKING GO?

_____
_____
_____
_____

WHEN/WHERE IS THE DATE?

_____
_____

HOW DID THE DATE GO?

_____
_____
_____
_____
_____
_____
_____

DO I WANT THERE TO BE A SECOND DATE?

_____

_____

_____

_____

_____

IF SO, WHAT WILL I DO ABOUT IT?

_____

_____

_____

_____

_____

HOW DID THE SECOND DATE GO?

_____

_____

_____

_____

_____

DATING RESOURCES FROM THE AUTHORS

BOOKS

Theology of His/Her Body
by Jason Evert

You: Life, Love, and the Theology of the Body
by Jason and Crystalina Evert

Chastity Is for Lovers: Single, Happy, and (Still) a Virgin
by Arleen Spenceley

Dating Detox: 40 Days of Perfecting Love in an Imperfect World
by Kevin and Lisa Cotter

Emotional Virtue: A Guide to Drama-Free Relationships
by Sarah Swafford

Forever: A Catholic Devotional for Your Marriage
by Jackie and Bobby Angel

How to Find Your Soulmate Without Losing Your Soul
by Jason and Crystalina Evert

If You Really Loved Me
by Jason Evert

Pure Manhood
by Jason Evert

Pure Womanhood
by Crystalina Evert

AUDIO

How to Date Your Soulmate
by Jason Evert

How to Save Your Marriage Before Meeting Your Spouse
by Jason Evert

Love or Lust?
by Jason and Crystalina Evert

Detox
by Jason Evert

Women Made New
by Crystalina Evert

WEBSITES

ascensionpress.com

chastityproject.com

womenmadenew.com

ACKNOWLEDGEMENTS

The Ascension team would like to thank the following people for their essential contributions to A *Guide to the Dating Project*:

- Pure Flix Studios, for producing *The Dating Project* film

- Tom Allen, for key promotion and distribution of the film

- Kerry Cronin, for creating the "dating assignment" featured in the film and in this Guide

- Jason and Crystalina Evert, for serving as invaluable lead authors of this Guide

- And for their unique perspectives and excellent contributions to this Guide:

    Bobby Angel
    Jackie Angel
    Kevin Cotter
    Jacinta Florence
    Paul J. Kim
    Fr. Mike Schmitz
    Arleen Spenceley
    Beth Sri
    Andrew Swafford